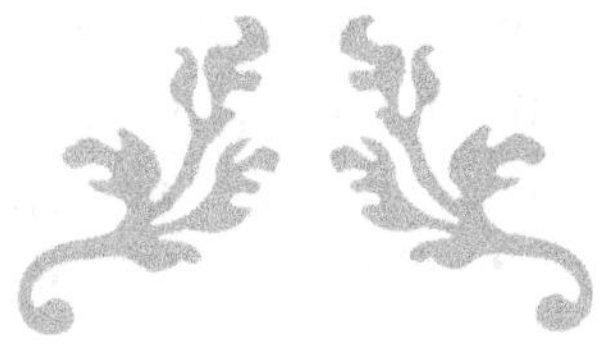

ECO-LIVING STARTS AT HOME

10 ways to go green today

Sheetal Kumar Niranjan

Dedication

To the pillars of my life,

G.A. Niranjan Kumar, my father, For your unwavering support and the strength you've instilled in me through your own example. You've taught me the value of hard work, integrity, resilience & to be a good family man.

P. Rajarathna, my mother, your boundless love, encouragement, and dedication to our family have been my guiding light. You've shown me the beauty of kindness, compassion and the importance of nurturing the mind and the heart.

N. Lakshmi, my sister, your endless enthusiasm and our unbreakable bond have been a constant source of inspiration. You've reminded me of the importance of joy, friendship, and family.

Vinutha S. Jain, my wife, your belief in me, patience, and unwavering partnership have been the bedrock of my journey. You've shown me the true meaning of love, partnership, and steadfast support.

Jia S. Jain, my daughter, you embody hope, the promise of a brighter future, and the reason for my endless determination. You've taught me the importance of legacy, responsibility, and the infinite possibilities of tomorrow.

This book is a tribute to your love, encouragement, and the countless moments we've shared. Because of your presence in my life, I've been able to embark on this journey. Thank you for being my constant source of strength and inspiration.

With all my love,

Sheetal Kumar Niranjan

Table of Contents

Introduction

"Green is the prime color of the world, and that from which its loveliness arises."

- Pedro Calderon de la Barca

The United Nations is a global organisation that works towards identifying and addressing global issues which apply to several countries. Two major problems that affect all of us are Climate Change and water, and both rank very high in the list of Global issues that the United Nations lists.

So, let's understand what exactly climate change is. In straightforward words, Climate change is simply the continuous rise in global temperatures, which is mainly the consequence of the increase in emissions of Green House gases and promoting the Green House effect

How is this impacting our planet and us? Climate change directly affects the Weather patterns, Production of Food, rise in sea levels & our health in general. To elaborate, we are constantly seeing a lot of untimely rainfall that's affecting our ability to get good yields from crops and causing disruption to agricultural practices. Rise in temperatures are causing bushfires and wiping out forest covers. Rising sea levels are causing more floods, typhoons and other natural calamities. Our health is adversely impacted due to the rise in pollution levels. All these challenges threaten our very existence, so we must act fast.

Source Image: by Kanenori from Pixabay.com

It is estimated that the next 30 years are very crucial for us to take action and to ensure that the rise in Global temperatures is maintained within 1.5 °C. If the temperatures are to rise by 1.5 °C, then the adverse impacts of Climate change will increase at an exponential rate.

It is well known that Carbon Dioxide CO2 is a major Greenhouse gas and that all significant steps being taken are to ensure that human-caused emissions of CO2 are constantly reduced each year so that it eventually reaches net-zero levels by 2050.

Now, this is a very ambitious goal, and all of us will have to do our bit to help attain it.

Let's understand the challenges around water now.

Reports from the United Nations mention that 40% of the world's population lives in countries or regions where water is scarce, and what's worse is that 80% of wastewater is left untreated, which means that it cannot be used. This lack of safe water leads to unhealthy sanitation practices. It becomes a significant threat to good health and well-being.

The scarcity of Drinking water is a massive problem in itself, especially in the Summer months of the year. Many of us rely on extracting underground water that's constantly depleting to alarmingly low levels, and we must do everything to conserve water and create more water sources simultaneously.

Waste handling and management is another huge problem. Incorrect practices in managing waste are leading to increased pollution levels in both land and water bodies and adversely affecting our lives and marine lives. Landfills are constantly being dumped with garbage and mostly with materials that are not biodegradable. Waste being dumped in water bodies doesn't help either. Remember that this waste that is not biodegradable is not going anywhere and is here to stay forever.

Eco-living and understanding it better is an excellent way to contribute towards reducing our carbon footprint and conserving water. This book will give you information on Eco-living and how you can begin by taking the proper steps to reduce our carbon footprints & save water, starting from home. Not only will you do your part to conserve our planet, but you will also do it in a pocket-friendly manner. So, let's dive into it.

1: Assessing the Environmental Impact

"Going green doesn't start with doing green acts, it starts with a shift in consciousness."

- Ian Somerhalder

While we are all eager to act immediately, knowing how we impact the environment through our lifestyle choices, behaviours, and activities is essential. The best way to do this is by measuring this impact, where various calculators for calculating carbon footprint, water footprint & waste footprint are handy.

I have used various calculators, which have helped me understand the multiple factors & areas where my contribution to carbon emissions is generally high. Some of these have also helped me understand water & waste management better, which was critical. With this information, I have researched and identified areas of improvement and have been taking remediation steps to reduce my footprint in these three crucial areas: Carbon, Water and waste footprints.

To get started, I recommend using the calculators mentioned below, as I describe them in some detail.

Measuring the carbon footprint

It is interesting to know how we are contributing to the CO2 emissions. The 3 Carbon Footprint calculators mentioned below will enlighten us through their questionaries.

The first one is from Saving nature, an organisation started in 2019 by Dr.Stuart Pimm. His vision is to restore nature for sustainable gains and to leave a broader environmental impact by taking action to restore habitats and ensure that biodiversity thrives.

You can access their calculator using the below URL:

https://savingnature.com/offset-your-carbon-footprint-carbon-calculator/

It will help understand your Total Annual CO2 emissions/year and give the number of trees that need to be planted to offset this CO2 footprint. I found this fascinating, and this very stat was a major eye-opener for me as it helped me understand the value of trees and the need for us to preserve them.

This 2nd calculator is made available by the Climate Change Department of the Government of Gujarat and is relevant for readers living in India. It will help identify the Total Carbon Footprint per household and person.

https://ccd.gujarat.gov.in/carbon-footprint-calculator.htm

This website also contains several details on reducing our carbon footprint, and it certainly introduced me to a concept called the "Carbon Handprint". Carbon Handprint is the brainchild of Gregory Norris, a lecturer at the Harvard School of Public Health, and this is a concept of taking all the positive actions that will help reduce the Carbon Footprint.

The 3rd calculator is one that the Government of India designed to calculate the CO2 emissions of vehicles that run on conventional fossil fuels and compare that against CO2 emissions of vehicles that run on electricity, namely electric vehicles. I know what you are thinking now: Electric vehicles generate CO2. What??? In a future chapter, I will explain this in detail, so stay intrigued.

https://e-amrit.niti.gov.in/co2-calculator

Measuring the water footprint

These calculators help us realise how much water we consume daily & how our behaviours and usage are leading to wastage, and how efficiently we can use it.

The 1st calculator is from the World Wildlife Fund – India, which is an organisation that is into the conservation of biodiversity & natural habitats.

http://watertales.wwfindia.org/water_footprint.php

This calculator helps understand the amount of direct & indirect consumption of water in litres/day. It also suggests how we could further reduce our water footprint, which I will mention in later chapters.

The 2nd calculator is from Water Footprint Network, a multi-stakeholder network that aims to facilitate fair and wise water use.

This calculator checks Food consumption and domestic water usage and gives the water footprint numbers.

Measuring the waste footprint

Waste disposal and management is such an important topic to pay attention to. The below-mentioned calculators help measure E-waste and plastic footprints.

The 1st calculator is created by WEEE4Future. They aim to Educate & raise awareness about E-waste and have made presentations and study material which anyone can use to educate themselves on E-waste.

This E-waste calculator is simply beautiful. It starts with asking us to play scavenger hunts in our homes and look for broken or unused gadgets. Then, we put in the number for each of the gadgets we found, and we got a score showing the amount of plastic and other toxic elements found in these gadgets. You will certainly love it.

The 2nd calculator is by Omni Calculator, a Polish start-up focusing on building custom calculators for their customers, including Plastic footprint calculators.

https://www.omnicalculator.com/ecology/plastic-footprint

This Plastic Footprint calculator takes input from the Kitchen supplies, bathroom and laundry, Disposable containers & packaging and provides the Plastic Footprint in terms of Kg/year. It also contains F.A.Q.s on Plastic Footprint and is a go-to tool for all information on Plastic waste and management.

Lastly, I recommend using all or most of these calculators to understand your Carbon, Water & waste footprint levels and keep them handy. You will likely use them as benchmark levels & over time, as you adopt the recommendations made in the later chapters, you should see these levels come down while your savings go up.

2: Reducing Energy Consumption

"The future will either be green or not at all."

- *Bob Brown*

India is the 3rd largest energy consumer in the world, with a need for over 200 Gigawatts of energy each month. The three primary energy sources have been Coal, Oil & Natural Gas, each belonging to the category of Fossil fuels. Thankfully, India's ability to generate more energy through Renewable and nuclear sources has increased steadily yearly.

The process of generating energy through Fossil fuels has adverse effects on the environment as it emits a lot of greenhouse gases, and that's never good. Therefore, as energy consumers, we should reduce our consumption and use energy more efficiently.

We can all take action to reduce energy consumption, even as you are reading this book. Think of when we have all left the light turned on in our bedrooms or the bathroom when nobody was in or using it—running the fan when we are not feeling hot. We had maybe left the T.V. on when nobody was watching it. These are all situations that all of us face every day. The first act for us could be as simple as turning off those lights, the T.V., the fan, or any other similar electric appliances when they are not required to be used. It is that simple. Trust me.

Now, let's get deeper into understanding more about energy-efficient lighting solutions and using smart home technologies that help us save and reduce energy consumption.

Energy-efficient lighting solutions

Traditional incandescent lights have been around for centuries and have been a critical component of our lighting solution options. Though these have served us very well, they are not as efficient, and they don't tend to last long as well. These lights consume up to 90% more energy and are hazardous to the environment. In most cases they are not disposed of appropriately once used.

It's great that as alternatives, there are several options now. You may have encountered L.E.D.,

C.F.L., or Halogen incandescent lights. These don't just last anywhere between 8x – 50x more than the Traditional incandescent lights but are very cost-effective in the long run. However, they are a little more expensive. They come in different sizes, shapes, wattage ratings and cover a wide range of the light spectrum of colours. Most importantly, these are cost-effective since they consume significantly less energy, sometimes as little as just ¼ the energy consumption of Traditional incandescent lights. These are used within homes and for lighting streets, traffic lamps, digital sign boards, etc.

Source Image: by Niek Verlaan from Pixabay.com

I also want to mention about motion sensor lights. These are lights that sense motion and stay on. However, they turn off after a stipulated time if there has been no movement or nobody is in a room or hall. These are fantastic and can save a lot of electricity.

Even if you look to replace the most frequently used Traditional incandescent lights within your home with these alternatives, you will reduce your electric bills as energy consumption comes down by up to 25% of our overall needs.

Utilising natural light effectively

What can be better than having our homes lit up by the natural light of the Sun? Not only does it help save energy and money, but it also helps keep our homes healthy and safe from insects and other disease-causing microbes. It also helps improve and maintain our overall health and keeps us active. It is also vital for our indoor plants to receive sunlight for them to flourish. Therefore, sunlight is essential to life in general.

To improve natural sunlight in homes, we could construct or renovate homes with more windows and use lighter shades of colours on the walls.

Keeping the windows clean is essential, too. Using thin curtains and drapes is good as they do not block most sunlight. You could install many mirrors so that sunlight reflects from them and reaches all corners of rooms, halls etc.

Smart home technologies for energy conservation

As a result of many technological advancements, we can make our homes smarter and reduce energy consumption.

Everyday appliances that use energy-efficient technologies, such as inverter technologies, save a lot of energy. Air Conditioners, refrigerators, fans, air coolers and many other appliances are manufactured using the inverter technology. Sales of such energy-efficient appliances are on the rise, and it is heartening to see such significant decisions being taken by consumers worldwide. The shopping decisions are also aided by Energy efficiency ratings provided as additional data for consumers and is something for all consumers to consider.

There are many smart devices such as smart lights, smart plugs, smart appliances, smart windows, smart thermostats and many more that one could use. Most of these have adopted the IoT technology to connect our homes and make them smart. All of these devices can be controlled through mobile apps, and you could even constantly monitor their usage through these apps. We could integrate all of our smart devices and control them on one app, which is very convenient.

We use a few smart bulbs & a smart plug that has helped us reduce energy consumption and save money. The smart bulbs especially are handy as they are essentially L.E.D. bulbs, and they give us the flexibility to choose the colour of the light along with its brightness. We typically use the White light and leave the brightness at around 30% as it is bright enough for us. The best part is that these smart bulbs help save an additional 50% of energy as soon as we lower the brightness to about 30%. Isn't that great!!!

The use of the smart plug has also been beneficial, as it helps convert many of our appliances to smart appliances. Using the timer feature, we can control the appliances by turning them on and off. We can control our Wi-Fi router and smart T.V., to name two such appliances/devices.

3: Harnessing Renewable Energy to generate electricity

"Being green and clean is not just an aspiration but an action."

- *Christine Pelosi*

The use of Renewable sources to generate electricity is gaining popularity mainly for the "clean" energy, which means there is no emission of any greenhouse gases. Additionally, we could save up to 90% of our electric bills by harnessing our natural resources and using them to generate electricity. Since these are available in abundance and are non-depleting sources, we do not have to worry about the supply of these resources ever coming down.

The most popular renewable energy sources for homes are Solar, Wind, and geothermal. I will mention more about each of these now.

Solar Energy

Source Image: by Photo Mix from Pixabay.com

Solar energy is generated by harnessing the Sun's rays to convert to electricity. For this, the installation of Solar panels is essential. Typically, the area available to place the solar panels on your terrace and the amount of electricity you are looking to generate become factors for understanding how many panels are needed. There are typically three types of systems – on-grid, off-grid, and hybrid. The on-grid system uses the central grid to store the electricity generated. In contrast, the off-grid system allows you to store the electricity generated within batteries for our consumption. The hybrid system is a combination of both systems. The Government of India makes the panels available at a subsidised cost, and steps have been shared to apply for this in https://solarrooftop.gov.in/.

On installation, you will receive a net meter, which will help determine the electricity consumed and generated by you. The difference units are then calculated by the electricity consumed – the electricity generated, and these differences in units are all that we will be billed for. While we bear the installation costs, you can expect to start getting returns from as early as within two years of installation.

Wind Energy

Source Image: by Marjon Besteman from Pixabay.com

You must have encountered huge wind turbines installed mostly atop hills and mountains. These generate electricity by using the kinetic energy of the wind, and they are so efficient that they generate electricity even when the rotor blades are rotating very slowly. Wind turbines come in different types, sizes and capacities.

Now, to harness the power of the wind right at our homes, smaller wind turbines can be easily installed on your rooftop or in your gardens. These wind turbines have a capacity of anywhere between a few hundred watts to tens of Kilowatts. One can invest based on the number of units of electricity to be generated. A wind turbine of 1KW capacity can produce about five units of electricity per day.

The generated electricity can be stored in grids just as in the case of electricity generated by Solar energy. The same three types of systems of on-grid, off-grid, and hybrid systems apply here as well. Using a net meter, you can pay for the difference units only if your energy consumption exceeds your energy generation.

Geothermal energy

Geothermal energy within homes is all about using Earth's natural heat to keep the temperatures at optimum levels within our homes and during all seasons throughout the year. Geothermal heat pumps are to be installed for us to harness the Earth's natural heat.

These Geothermal systems are suitable substitutes for traditional Air conditioners as they help consume less electricity and save money. Though these are less popular than the other renewable energy options, they are gaining prominence as consumers become aware of this option for creating clean energy.

4: Water Conservation Practices

"Green is a process, not a status. We need to think of 'green' as a verb, not an adjective. "

- Daniel Goleman

The importance of water conservation is well documented and spoken about very frequently & very rightly so. Lack of potable water is such a huge issue in most countries. Only about 3% of water is freshwater, of which about only 1% of it is available. About 2% of it is stored within glaciers and ice caps. With just 1% of it being available for the entire planet to consume and use, it is needless to say that fresh water is such a scarce commodity.

Water sources to homes are typically of 2 kinds, namely groundwater & surface water. Groundwater is stored within porous rocks a few meters in the ground and can be extracted by digging wells. Surface water is typically available within rivers, lakes and reservoirs. Groundwater within wells is drying up quickly as the reserves get empty, and the rise in temperatures only quickens the process. As for surface water, these are getting contaminated as domestic and industrial waste is added to them, making it a challenging and expensive process to decontaminate and use.

Therefore, the onus is on us to refrain from polluting our water bodies, to use water wisely and not waste this precious commodity.

Implementing water-efficient fixtures

To conserve water at home, we need to install water-efficient fixtures. These could be related to Bathroom fixtures, Kitchen fixtures or even R.O. Water Purifiers.

Bathroom Fixtures

Fixtures within bathrooms, such as Wash basins, health faucets, showers, taps, toilets and bathtubs, dispense water as and when we use them. If these are not used correctly or if we do not have any of them functioning properly, it could lead to severe wastage of water.

Low-flow aerators & showerheads

Water-saving Aerators are devices that easily fit into Wash basin taps, regular taps & faucets and help control the water flow while ensuring the same water pressure is maintained. These devices come in different sizes and with different water flow rates and are very handy in reducing water usage. Some aerators help save up to 80% of water.

Flow restrictors are used when aerators cannot be installed as a device in taps or faucets. These restrictors can help save up to 60% of water and are available for different flow rates.

A low-flow showerhead is an excellent option for a showerhead as it is designed to help reduce water use during a shower. There is no compromise on the pressure of the water and the shower experience, and it can help save up to 60% of water when compared with using a regular shower. Water flows at about 8 litres/min while using a low-flow showerhead and at a rate of 20 litres/min while using a regular showerhead. So, for a 10 mins shower, we are looking at saving about 120 litres of water.

Dual Flush Toilets

While toilets come in different sizes and have various water-holding capacities within the tanks, it is also good to opt for one that allows us to use a partial or full flush. These options are present in Dual flush toilets, and they help save about 40% of flushing water when used wisely. Some toilets also use Tank banks that can help reduce up to 2 litres of water per flush.

Kitchen fixtures

Faucets and Taps in kitchens are used to dispense water. In the case of Bathroom fixtures, low-flow aerators are great devices that can be used to control the rate of water flow and save water subsequently.

R.O. Water purifiers

The choice of water purifiers or filters is of utmost importance. Not only does it help us cleanse and remove toxins from water so that it is fit for drinking, but it also helps determine how much water is discarded during filtration.

R.O. water purifiers are the best in getting rid of contaminants and very minute particles that cause harm to the body. The reverse osmosis process helps purify water to that degree. However, the downside is that a lot of wastewater carrying the contaminants does need to be drained out.

However, the amount of wastewater depends on the desired level of T.D.S. [Total dissolved solids] set within the R.O. water purifier. The lower the T.D.S. level, the higher the purity of water, and the more the amount of wastewater drained out. Therefore, T.D.S. levels are to be set higher, typically above 150, to ensure that the purity of water is maintained as well as the amount of wastewater generated is lowered.

Rainwater harvesting

Rainwater harvesting is a prevalent practice these days, and we can see a lot of promotion of this from government agencies all over the world. New homes, residential apartments, and even commercial properties are finding ways to create systems that facilitate rainwater harvesting.

Rainwater harvesting helps reduce our water bills as reliance on conventional water supply could be reduced. Rainwater harvesting is sometimes a lifeline for towns or cities that face water scarcity. The harvested water can be stored and used during drought or dry seasons. Rainwater harvesting helps boost groundwater levels.

Rainwater harvesting is simply collecting and storing rainwater after filtering or treating it as part of the purification process. Collection of water typically happens from rooftops or open grounds. This water can then be used for watering plants or other domestic uses.

It is important to understand the main components of a rainwater harvesting system so we can adopt and create a rainwater harvesting system for our use.

- Catchment – is the terrace surface or the open ground that acts as the rainwater collecting system.
- Transportation – Water pipes or drains that can be used to move the collected water to the storage or filtration unit come under this component.
- First flush – is a mechanism of removing water and not storing it after the first rain, as the catchment area would often contain a lot of pollutants or debris that would need to get cleaned up, which occurs organically right after the first rain. Water collection can start from the second rain.
- Filter – is used to clean the rainwater and treat it to make it usable.

Source Image: by Manfred Antranias Zimmer from
Pixabay.com

Rainwater Harvesting Techniques & Methods

Rainwater harvesting methods can be broadly classified into two, namely, harvesting surface rainwater & harvesting rooftop rainwater.

- Harvesting surface rainwater includes techniques allowing groundwater to be collected in different storage units.
- Harvesting rooftop rainwater includes techniques that allow rainwater on rooftops to be collected in different storage units.

The storage units include tanks, borewells, recharge pits & shaft recharge harvesting wells. The techniques used to facilitate storage are mainly percolation, in which water moves down the soil and collects in the storage unit and trenches, in which water passes through ditches and drain pipes.

5: Waste Reduction and Recycling

I am in love with this green Earth.

~ *Charles Lamb*

Waste generation and its management have been an area of concern for many nations across the globe. While the generation of waste is easy, its appropriate disposal and recycling is crucial and difficult in most cases. The simplest way to think of waste is something that we do not need anymore or cannot be used anymore, whether it is food, clothes, plastics, other packaging materials or even electronic appliances & gadgets. On the flip side, waste can also be seen as a treasure by some, especially waste management companies that have well-matured processes and techniques to manage and recycle waste.

It also becomes our responsibility to reduce the waste we generate at home and look for opportunities to recycle them. At the least, it is essential to segregate waste and dispose of them appropriately.

Setting up an efficient home Waste segregation & recycling system

Local governing bodies and sanitation departments have made waste segregation mandatory in some cities & countries. It should be more of a choice we all adopt and practice irrespective of any mandate.

Waste segregation at home is critical as it ensures that we segregate waste based on certain types of waste, such as wet, dry, bio or sanitary, hazardous, inert or e-waste. This segregation helps prevent waste from unnecessarily being dumped in landmines when it could have been appropriately treated, recycled, or disposed of properly without harming the environment. This simple step also ensures that the job of the waste collectors is made simple, and they do not have to put their health at risk.

Let's understand the types of waste in detail to understand what needs to be done with it.

- Wet waste is typically produced by food waste, fruit & vegetable waste and any other waste that's produced in the kitchen. These are biodegradable and make for great material to produce compost.

- Dry waste typically consists of dry materials such as cloth, paper, wood, rubber, plastic, glass or metals. This type of waste can largely be recycled.
- Bio or sanitary waste is generated from hospitals, clinics, laboratories, and human or animal excreta. These are to be disposed of carefully by following proper sanitation treatment practices.
- Hazardous waste – Wastes that threaten our health, such as toxic gases, pesticides, batteries, fireworks, poisons, and radioactive material, among others. Safe disposal is of utmost importance.
- E-waste comprises of discarded electronic devices or gadgets and all associated accessories. These can be looked to be refurbished or recycled.
- Inert waste – Waste that does not react to chemicals or is not biodegradable, or decomposes at a prolonged rate, such as construction waste of sand, rock, debris and concrete. Recycling and recreating the original material, such as bricks or concrete blocks, is the best option.

What do we do with waste that can be recycled?

Well, there are so many options. It all begins with the first step of segregating the waste and then choosing the disposal options listed below.

- You can choose to give waste away to the waste collectors that are assigned by local municipal authorities.
- These days, several start-ups are looking for particular types of waste that they use to recycle and create usable products. You could choose to sell waste to them.
- You could sell plastic or glass waste to private waste collectors.
- Manufacturers of products do collect back the packaging material or their discarded products for a buyback or refund price.
- You could choose to make D.I.Y. crafts.
- Clothes can be donated.
- You can compose waste to create soil rich in nutrients and use them for gardening.

Composting organic waste

Source Image: by Manfred Antranias Zimmer from Pixabay.com

Composting is a process in which organic waste can naturally decompose and become nutritionally rich fertilisers and soil boosters for plants and trees. Food and other organic waste are a significant percentage of the overall waste generated in homes. With the chosen composting method, we can have good quality compost available spanning within a few weeks to a few years.

There are two main types of composting methods for homes, namely, cold composting and hot composting.

Cold Composting

Often referred to as passive composting, this method is simply about letting organic waste decompose independently without any intervention. Nature takes its course, and microorganisms break down the waste in predominantly an oxygen-less environment. Since this method takes years to produce compost, it is preferred only when there is less organic waste to produce compost from. The produced compost may contain a lot of pathogens or parasites and could be pretty smelly and wet.

Hot composting

Often referred to as active composting, this method is more of the monitored and managed approach of producing compost. Organic waste is stored in a controlled environment in high temperatures where carbon & nitrogen levels are maintained at optimum levels. Water also ensures that an oxygen-rich environment is created, attracting more organisms that break down the organic waste. This method helps generate compost within a few weeks to a few months. High temperatures also ensure that parasites or pathogens don't thrive. The compost is, hence, less smelly & dry.

Creating nutrient-rich compost for your garden

To create an ecosystem for composting, we must ensure that the compost pile or compost bins are about 9 sq. feet to 25 sq. feet in dimensions. These piles and bins could be kept inside of your home or outside. It is often preferred to be kept outside as the conditions would aid in producing compost sooner. If you prefer the cold composting method, producing compost could take years. Hot composting would produce compost in a few weeks to a few months.

While we were introduced to both composting methods a little while back, it will be nice to understand Hot composting more in detail.

Hot composting elements such as Carbon, Nitrogen, air & water are essential. Sources of carbon & nitrogen are often the waste that is produced. Rich carbon sources can be small pieces of paper or cardboard, dead leaves or twigs, to name a few. Rich nitrogen sources include dairy waste, coffee filters or tea bags, fruits & vegetable waste and grass clippings.

It is vital to maintain the proper carbon-to-nitrogen ratio, usually between 20 to 30 parts of carbon for every 1 part of nitrogen, to maintain the high temperatures of around 50 to 60 ° C or 125 to 140 ° F, so that micro and macro organisms are attracted and participate in most actively breaking down the waste.

This ecosystem requires constant monitoring to ensure that all conditions are maintained for compost production. A fall in temperatures could mean that parasites and pathogens are allowed to thrive, and the final product contains these parasites and pathogens and is quite smelly and wet. On the other hand, if temperatures rise above optimal levels, the compost will be left nutrient-deficient and very dry.

I hope that this gives you sufficient information to start producing your compost.

6: Embracing Eco-Friendly Personal hygiene products & Cleaning products

"If there is a future, it will be Green."

- Petra Kelly

We use personal hygiene & cleaning products every day in our lives. They certainly exist in many shapes & forms and can be categorised based on what we use them for. Regarding personal hygiene products, we use soaps, toothpaste and brushes, bathing & shower gels, shampoos, wipes, and sanitisers, to name most of them. Cleaning products include cleaners for toilets, bathrooms, glass, floors, cars, and clothes, among others. Most of these products contain chemicals that can cause harm due to their toxic or polluting nature.

Eco-friendly cleaning is all about using personal hygiene & cleaning products that are free from harmful chemicals that could potentially harm us or our planet. Thanks to the research and hard work of people and organisations looking to create sustainable products, we can find a wide range of such products now.

Transitioning to using eco-friendly personal hygiene & cleaning products

The most important step to take to start using eco-friendly personal hygiene & cleaning products is not only to unquestioningly believe in what we are fed as information but to invest some time to educate and research the ingredients used and also to be aware of whether the products are manufactured in an eco-friendly manner. We should also look for certifications or product approvals from the concerned administrations & governing bodies. Other factors to consider would be from a packaging and distribution standpoint. Packaging material that can be recycled is usually the preferred choice of eco-friendly products.

We could replace one product at a time and not replace them all at once. That way, we get time to adjust to these products while understanding how they need to be used. We will also need to be aware of how to properly store these products & dispose of them once they are used.

Natural alternatives to chemical cleaners

Many natural alternatives to chemical cleaners are readily available and very budget-friendly. Such popular alternatives are Baking Soda, Lemon juice, vinegar, Oils, starch, hydrogen peroxide, castile soap & salt.

Let's understand their applications now.

- Baking soda – By mixing with water, we can use the paste to scrub sinks & stove tops due to their deodorising & mildly abrasive nature.
- Lemon juice – This is a natural disinfectant, and due to its ability to break down grease, it can be used on surfaces that need the removal of stains or general sanitisation.
- Vinegar – Can be used as an all-purpose cleaner to clean bathroom surfaces, kitchen countertops or glass surfaces. Its acidic properties help dissolve grease or other deposits. They do not smell bad, either.
- Oils – Coconut oil can be used to remove residue that's sticky and helps clean and polish stainless steel appliances. Olive oil is excellent to use for polishing wooden furniture. Essential oils are great additives to cleaning solutions due to their antimicrobial properties.
- Starch – Can be used to clean glass and to shine surfaces.

- Hydrogen Peroxide – Can be used in place of bleaches for disinfectant & stain removal, especially in bathroom surfaces and kitchen countertops.
- Castile soap – It's made of vegetable oils and can be used as laundry detergent, washing dishes and as a floor cleaner.
- Salt – Can be used to remove tough stains from utensils and kitchen surfaces due to its abrasive nature.

Several recipes can be created and used by these very same ingredients. They must be mixed in the right proportion and tested before use. The internet can provide many recipes for creating these cleaners for each specific purpose.

During my research, I have encountered certain safety considerations to be followed while creating, storing & using these cleaners.

- It's always good to store each specific cleaner in separate bottles, use one bottle for a particular cleaner, and reuse it to store only that cleaner.
- Do not mix vinegar with hydrogen peroxide or bleach, as the mixture creates fumes that could be toxic.
- Mix bleach with only water and nothing else.
- Ensure to wear proper safety equipment such as gloves and masks.

7: Sustainable Home Construction & Renovations

"I think any opportunity you have to be green, whether it's in business or in everyday life, you should take it."

- Lauren Conrad

Building sustainable homes means constructing homes in an environmentally friendly manner by taking actions that ensure the use of practices & materials that are sustainable and don't cause much harm to our planet.

Various aspects need to be considered for building a sustainable home or renovating the home, such as ensuring energy efficiency, good water conservation systems, green building material selections & efficient use of them without wastage, proper ventilation systems, passive design strategy to ensure natural resources are better utilised, installing smart devices and weather resilient construction. While a few of these have already been mentioned in earlier chapters, I will cover the other important aspects in this chapter.

Green building materials selections

Choosing the right building materials is crucial to building a long-lasting and sustainable home. With the proper use of these materials in construction & renovation work, the energy efficiency of homes can be enhanced. Governments across nations promote the construction of sustainable buildings and even provide certificates to these "Green Buildings".

Source Image: by Steve Buissinne from Pixabay.com

Here are some construction materials with the benefits of using them

1) Recycled materials such as recycled steel, reclaimed wood, recycled glass, and recycled

concrete help reduce waste in landfills and conserve natural resources.

2) Wood from forests that are managed in an environmentally responsible and socially beneficial manner helps reduce deforestation. It promotes practices that lead to sustainable management of forests.

3) Low volatile organic compound [V.O.C.s] paints & adhesives help maintain good indoor air quality, as the emission of harmful gases from V.O.C.s chemicals is negated to a large extent. Natural low V.O.C. materials such as clay and lime are good for plasters and finishers and can be used as wall finishes.

4) Insulation materials such as cellulose, recycled denim, and spray foam are deemed High-performance insulation materials, and this helps maintain consistent temperatures indoors, thereby reducing the need for additional heating or cooling, which leads to efficient use of electricity. Solar reflective Paints & coatings provide similar benefits as well.

5) Fly Ash, used as a partial replacement for concrete, helps reduce the need for cement. Reduction of cement use means lowered carbon emissions during the production of cement.

6) Bamboo and Cork can be used as replacements for wood. These are harvested in a very sustainable manner and are sturdy

enough to provide strength to buildings. These make for good flooring materials.

7) Permeable pavers & gravel can be used at suitable places to help facilitate the process of rainwater harvesting.

8) Earthen materials such as mud, grass, straw, stones & rocks can be used to provide strength & good insulation for homes.

9) Recycled plastic bricks and eco-bricks have also been commonly used as construction materials. These can be used for building roofing and walls.

10) Biocomposites and bioplastics are gaining popularity as well. Roots of mushrooms known as mycelium are being used as insulation material.

11) Precast concrete slabs are also eco-friendly, as they are manufactured in controlled factory conditions, increasing their durability.

Enhancing energy efficiency with windows and doors

Climate conditions & building needs that demand Glazing efficiency, improved insulation, ventilation needs and thermal efficiency require the right choices of materials & construction designs and methods for constructing Windows and doors. Energy-efficient windows and doors help reduce electric bills as energy consumption is lowered.

Below are some key points to consider for enhancing energy efficiency with windows and doors.

1) Selection of Windows – Windows with high-performance glazing and low-emissivity coatings are great options. Multiple panes of glass are good for improving insulation.
2) The right Frame materials – Composite, Polyvinyl chloride, fibreglass, wood-clad & aluminium make for energy-efficient frame materials. These materials have good insulation properties and are thermal resistant.
3) Ensuring the windows and doors are correctly installed, as sealing and insulation around the frames are essential to prevent air leaks and minimise drafts. Subsequently, cracks, gaps or openings will need to be filled as and when they appear.
4) Appropriate shades, blinds & curtains are to be used based on the climate conditions.
5) Doors with high thermal resistance & an insulated core are good choices.
6) Regular maintenance & replacement of old doors or windows helps maintain energy efficiency.
7) Smart windows & doors are exciting options for the near future.
8) You can consider windows & doors with high energy efficiency ratings and look for incentives or tax rebates on some of these installations that might help reduce costs,

8: Sustainable Transportation Choices

"You could cover the whole earth with asphalt, but sooner or later green grass would break through."

- Ilya Ehrenburg

Transportation accounts for about 25%-30% of total greenhouse gas emissions. Greenhouse gases such as Carbon Dioxide [CO2], Carbon Monoxide [C.O.], Methane[CH4], Nitrous Oxide[N2O], Hydroflurocarbons[HFC] & particulate matter are primarily emitted by vehicles, of which about 24% of emissions are Carbon Dioxide alone. These are high numbers, and this is a huge problem.

Thankfully, where there are problems, there are opportunities to build sustainable solutions, and several solutions have been developed and continue to evolve.

As the burning of fossil fuels is the leading cause of emissions of Greenhouse gases in vehicles, a lot of research and development has been carried out to build engines that consume alternative fuels such as electricity, hydrogen fuel cells and compressed natural gas [C.N.G.]. These have proven their efficiency and are beneficial in reducing Greenhouse gas emissions. Adoption of such vehicles is on the rise, and that's great to see.

An argument could be made that electric vehicles require electricity to run, and the electricity generation predominantly involves fossil fuels, leading to Greenhouse gas emissions. While this is accurate, electric vehicle usage cuts down Greenhouse gas emissions more than it is responsible for generating the same.

While opting to use vehicles that run on Alternative fuels, simple lifestyle changes and wiser choices made by us could go a long way in helping reduce Greenhouse gases. Let's explore these options one by one.

Reducing our reliance on cars

Cars are a necessity for most households today. We all have our own reasons for owning a car, which are often justified. Cars help us commute from one place to another and offer flexibility in travel scheduling. The need for safe and comfortable travel is also a reason for using a car. However, most Greenhouse emissions by vehicles are primarily due to using cars.

Reduction of usage of cars is essential for many reasons such as lowering Greenhouse gas emissions, avoiding traffic congestion & improving public health.

So, how can we reduce our usage of cars? Here goes.

- Walking or cycling to cover short distances.
- Carpooling to reduce the number of single-occupancy vehicles on the road.
- Use public transportation such as busses, local trains, metro rails, cabs & autorickshaws.
- Finding opportunities to avoid commuting, such as remotely working from home, using technology to conduct meetings online and avoiding travel for a face-to-face meeting.
- Allowing flexible work hours helps avoid rush hour traffic as vehicles in traffic jams burn more fuel.
- Using vehicles that use alternative fuel such as electricity, hydrogen fuel cells or C.N.G.
- Using car-sharing services such as car rentals or borrowing cars reduces individual car ownership.

All of this definitely needs the right infrastructure and urban planning & development within cities & towns, and thankfully, most authorities & governing bodies realise this and are working constantly to help address these needs.

Transitioning to electric vehicles

Source Image: by Marilyn Murphy from Pixabay.com

Transitioning to electric vehicles is a good step towards reducing our carbon footprint. Before transitioning to using E.V. vehicles, it is important to research the available E.V. vehicles and understand their features, charging requirements, cost, insurance options & mileage, i.e., the number of miles or kilometres the vehicle can travel in a single charge.

Cost often plays a crucial in us making our decisions. Though it may look expensive, the returns are much higher than regular fossil fuel-run vehicles. Government incentives & rebates help promote the sales of these vehicles, which has been a great step and aid in lowering the cost of the vehicle such that it is available at a subsidised price.

Charging requirement is key as the vehicle may need a level 2 home charger. Not only this, charging points made available for use by the public are equally crucial to ensure there are enough charging points at various locations in the city. E.V. vehicles with good mileage or range can be considered as well.

Insurance options play a vital role. The insurance provider must be consulted to understand the terms and conditions for insuring an E.V. vehicle.

Selling existing vehicles is a thing to consider before buying the E.V. vehicle.

9: Green Landscaping and Gardening

"For in the true nature of things, if we rightly consider, every green tree is far more glorious than if it were made of gold and silver."

- Martin Luther

Home gardening, as we all know, is about growing plants and trees within a plot of land or around our homes to create a green cover that is not only good for the environment but also benefits us by improving air quality and growing fruits and vegetables that we can consume. Landscaping helps us design these gardens and use natural elements like rocks, fountains, or small ponds to enhance the aesthetic appearance.

Source Image: by F. Muhammad from Pixabay.com

Green landscaping and gardening practices help us preserve and facilitate the healthy growth of these plants, trees and other natural elements while eliminating or reducing any harmful environmental effects caused by improper landscaping and gardening methods.

Some of the ways to practice green landscaping and gardening approaches are as follows:

- Growing native plants & trees that easily adapt to the local climate and atmospheric conditions and ones that require less maintenance. These use less fertilisers and water for growth and provide us with food.
- Following Organic gardening practices, synthetic fertilisers are replaced with compost or organic fertilisers. These not only enrich the

soil and improve its health but also eliminate toxic chemicals from being used.

- Other practices that help improve soil health include mulching, contour farming techniques, reducing soil compaction and preventing soil erosion.
- Using water efficiently by implementing drip irrigation and rainwater harvesting to preserve and use water efficiently.
- Reduce the lawn area as it requires high maintenance and consumes a lot of water. Instead, plants & trees can be planted in such a way that they provide good shade and benefit from low water consumption and energy efficiency.
- Using sustainable construction materials to construct structures such as walkways and garden beds.
- Follow pest management techniques that do not require the use of harmful chemicals. These techniques include installing traps to catch harmful flies and insects, crop rotation to facilitate the growth of in-season plants & trees and attracting birds & beneficial insects by installing water features & feeders.
- Following Permaculture approaches that focus on landscape designing that is inspired by flourishing natural ecosystems.
- Growing vertical gardens and using rooftops & balconies to grow gardens. They improve air quality and help improve the look of plain buildings.

Hopefully, this aligns our thoughts towards making environmentally responsible choices when constructing gardens.

10: Fostering Eco-Conscious Habits

"Nature's first green is gold. "

- Robert Frost

The motivation and the need to lead an Eco-conscious lifestyle and to cultivate habits that help us lead this lifestyle should come from within. We should feel the need to contribute to "Go Green" in our ways, and hopefully, the preceding chapters were filled with valuable information that can be used to make these lifestyle changes.

Some fundamental behavioural changes to adopt Eco-Conscious habits are:

1. Educating ourselves by understanding the existing environmental issues and challenges and researching them to take actionable steps will help us reduce them, if not eliminate them. Through this book, I have made a humble attempt to mention and address these issues to minimise the negative impact we cause and leave behind on the environment.
2. Opting for sustainable transportation, carpooling and sharing.
3. "Reduce, Reuse and recycle" is perhaps the most important tagline to live with for anyone

thats keen on promoting sustainable living. The simplest way to describe it is by stating, Reduce to leave no waste behind and to ensure that we only buy what we truly need and use. Reuse is to ensure that we continue to use items or things until they become unusable. Recycling is ensuring that things or items made of recyclable materials are either repurposed or handed out to organisations that can create other items made from these recycled materials. Paper, plastics & glass are a few materials that can be recycled.

4. Conserving energy & water. Opting for generating energy using renewable energy sources such as solar panels to harness solar energy and reduce electricity bills.

5. Replacing single-use plastics with items made from other sustainable materials such as cloth, stainless steel, glass, bamboo, etc. There are many alternatives to find these days, and it would be great to support the makers of such products by promoting them and buying them.

6. Practising mindful consumerism, which we will go over in detail shortly.

7. Switching to a vegetarian diet that promotes plant-based diet rather than an animal-based diet would help reduce greenhouse gases significantly. Reducing food waste is another essential step.

8. Green landscaping and gardening and growing our food.

9. Volunteer in community & workplace-driven activities that conduct clean-up and afforestation drives.
10. Practicing what we preach and staying well-informed is vital. Through examples that we set, we can inspire everyone else around us and be great advocates of change for the betterment of our environment.

We should adopt these habits and do it slowly but deliberately and not rush through it. It is vital to stay at it by being persistent and remembering that every small effort goes a long way in making a difference.

Source Image: by Tomasz Mikolajczyk from Pixabay.com

Being a mindful consumer

Being a mindful consumer is all about making choices that are well thought about such that there is no excess purchasing and being aware to ensure sustainability is promoted.

Here are a few steps that we could take to be mindful consumers.

1) Being clear about why we need to buy something is essential. If the reason for buying something justifies the need and aligns with our values, then it is a right buy. This clarity also helps prevent impulsive buying as we know what to buy.
2) Researching the products we buy and looking for information on whether they are made ethically and are sustainable. The claims are usually supported by certifications and information that is publicly available.
3) Buying quality products rather than falling prey to the quantity of products of substandard quality is essential.
4) Buying second-hand good quality products helps reuse products. It can also prove to be less expensive than buying a new product.
5) Avoid buying single-use items to avoid generating more waste. Opting for reusable alternatives is the way to go.
6) Practising Minimalism by decluttering and keeping just the essentials is a necessary

mindset. It is, however, challenging to follow and needs firm resolve to maintain this lifestyle.

7) Repairing and using refurbished products can help prevent unnecessary buying of new replacement products.

8) Buying locally made products & using local services is excellent as the logistics around procurement and transportation become so much easier and leave behind smaller environmental footprints.

9) Looking for products with minimal packaging and use of sustainable materials is good.

Conclusion

Wow. What a thrilling journey it has been to write this book and share my knowledge and learnings with you. I truly appreciate that you are willing to take steps to ensure that you do your bit and contribute to making our planet more sustainable. I hope this book has given you enough information to start your eco-living journey.

I would also encourage you to do in-depth research in any or all of the ten ways & more by which you can "Go Green" right from home and pass that knowledge on to your family and friends. Remember, together, we can make our planet more sustainable.

Thank you for reading through the entire book and wishing you well in your eco-living journey.

Bibliography

The United Nations (2023).
https://www.un.org/en/global-issues/climate-change

National Geographic (2017). Causes and Effects of Climate Change.
https://www.youtube.com/watch?v=G4H1N_yXBiA

The United Nations (2023).
https://www.un.org/en/global-issues/water

Anisha Shashidharan & Sanjay Arya (2022). India Country commercial Guide - Energy. International Trade Administration.
https://www.trade.gov/country-commercial-guides/india-energy

Rinkesh Kukreja (2023). What are Most Common Energy Efficient Lighting Types?. Conserve Energy Future. https://www.conserve-energy-future.com/energy-efficient-lighting-types.php

9 BENEFITS OF HAVING NATURAL LIGHTING IN THE HOME(2021). Shea Homes.
https://www.sheahomes.com/blog/9-benefits-of-having-natural-lighting-in-the-home/

How to Use Smart Home Technology to Increase Energy efficiency in Your Home (2023). HDL Automation. https://www.hdlautomation.com/Articles_100000158316716.html#:~:text=By%20using%20smart%20thermostats%2C%20lighting,money%20on%20your%20utility%20bills.

Lora Shinn (2022). Renewable Energy: The Clean Facts. Natural Resources Defense Council. https://www.nrdc.org/stories/renewable-energy-clean-facts#sec-whatis

Tanu Shreee (2023). "Harnessing Renewable Energy at Home: Simple Tips for a Sustainable Future". Linkedin. https://www.linkedin.com/pulse/harnessing-renewable-energy-home-simple-tips-future-tanuu-shree

Ecoideaz (2016). A Wind Turbine Now For Homes in India. Ecoideaz.com. https://www.ecoideaz.com/eco-news-india/a-wind-turbine-now-for-homes-in-india#:~:text=Avant%20Garde%20Innovations%20(AGI)%2C,may%20cost%20around%20INR50%2C000.

Energy.gov(2023). Installing and Maintaining a small wind electric system. Energy.gov.

https://www.energy.gov/energysaver/installing-and-maintaining-small-wind-electric-system

Bureau of Reclamation California-Great Basin(2020). Water Facts - Worldwide Water Supply. Usbr.gov. https://www.usbr.gov/mp/arwec/water-facts-ww-water-sup.html#:~:text=Water%20covers%20about%2071%25%20of%20the%20earth's%20surface.&text=97%25%20of%20the%20earth's%20water,most%20industrial%20uses%20except%20cooling).&text=3%25%20of%20the%20earth's%20water%20is%20fresh.

Econaur (2023). Water Conservation Technique – Product that Reduces Water Use in Building. Econaur.com. https://econaur.com/water-conservation-methods-using-products-that-reduce-water-use-in-buildings/

Umar Shareef (2023). Water Purifiers types, Which water purifier should buy. Zelect.in. https://www.zelect.in/water-purifier/water-purifier-types

Housing News Desk (2023). Rain water harvesting: Importance, techniques, pros and cons. Housing.com. https://housing.com/news/different-rain-water-harvesting-methods/

Team Greensutra(2023). Waste Segregation: All you need to know. Greensutra.in. https://greensutra.in/waste-segregation-all-you-need-to-know/

Shelia Hu (2020). Composting 101. Nrdc.org. https://www.nrdc.org/stories/composting-101#types

Colleen Vanderlinden & Kathleen Miller (2022). Hot Composting: How to Make Compost in Less Time. Thespruce.com. https://www.thespruce.com/how-to-hot-compost-2539474

Debra Rose Wilson & Ashley Hubbard (2022). 18 Easy and Green DIY Recipes to Clean All the Things, Plus Health Benefits. Healthline.com. https://www.healthline.com/health/easy-green-diy-recipes-to-clean-all-the-things-plus-health-benefits#supplies

Vikram Singh(2014). Green Building Materials. Architecture – Time, Space & People. Council of Architecture, India. https://www.coa.gov.in/show_img.php?fid=137

Rinkesh Kukreja (2023). 17+ Sustainable and Green Building Construction Materials. Conserve Energy Future. https://www.conserve-energy-future.com/sustainable-construction-materials.php

About the Author

Sheetal Kumar Niranjan is an Indian Author, an eco-enthusiast and an I.T. professional with 15 years of experience. He currently works at Tesco Bengaluru as a Systems Engineer. He holds a Master's degree in Electrical Engineering from State University of New York, New Paltz, U.S.A. and a Bachelor's degree in Electronics and Communication Engineering from B.M.S. Institute of Technology, Bangalore, India.

He loves to explore food and try different delicacies from various cuisines. An avid sports lover and enthusiast, he likes to both watch and play sports. He loves playing cricket and foosball. He also loves to travel and watch movies that inspire him. His recent interest has been in researching and learning about climate change and the impact it's causing around the world. Through this book, shares the same learnings and knowledge with his readers.

You can reach out to him at sheetalkumarn@gmail.com with your reviews and thoughts.